CRAYOLA
WILD WORLD
OF ANIMAL
COLORS

Laura Purdie Salas

Lerner Publications ◆ Minneapolis

For Capt. Jack Sparrow, Oreo, Annie, Muffin, Peaches, Peppy, Sweet Pea, Zorro, and all the animals—domestic and wild—that have added color, joy, and love to our family

Lerner Publications Company
A division of Lerner Publishing Group, Inc.
241 First Avenue North
Minneapolis, MN 55401 USA

For reading levels and more information, look up this title at www.lernerbooks.com.

Main body text set in Billy Infant Semibold 19/26.
Typeface provided by SparkyType.

Library of Congress Cataloging-in-Publication Data

Names: Salas, Laura Purdie, author.
Title: Crayola wild world of animal colors / Laura Purdie Salas.
Description: Minneapolis : Lerner Publications, [2018] | Audience: Age 6-9. | Audience: K to grade 3. | Includes bibliographical references and index.
Identifiers: LCCN 2017038773 (print) | LCCN 2017042128 (ebook) | ISBN 9781541512412 (lb : alk. paper) | ISBN 9781541526723 (pb : alk. paper) | ISBN 9781541512573 (eb pdf)
Subjects: LCSH: Animals—Color—Juvenile literature. | Protective coloration (Biology)—Juvenile literature. | Camouflage (Biology)—Juvenile literature. | Crayons—Juvenile literature.
Classification: LCC QL767 .S2427 2018 (print) | LCC QL767 (ebook) | DDC 590—dc23

LC record available at https://lccn.loc.gov/2017038773

Manufactured in the United States of America
2-47052-34004-12/20/2018

TABLE OF CONTENTS

ANIMAL COLORS EVERYWHERE

Animals come in many colors. Yellow canaries. Orange foxes. Blue fish.

Sometimes one animal has all the colors of a rainbow! This panther chameleon is bright blue or lime green, until it feels threatened.

Then it turns yellow, orange, or fiery red!

Animals use colors in amazing ways.

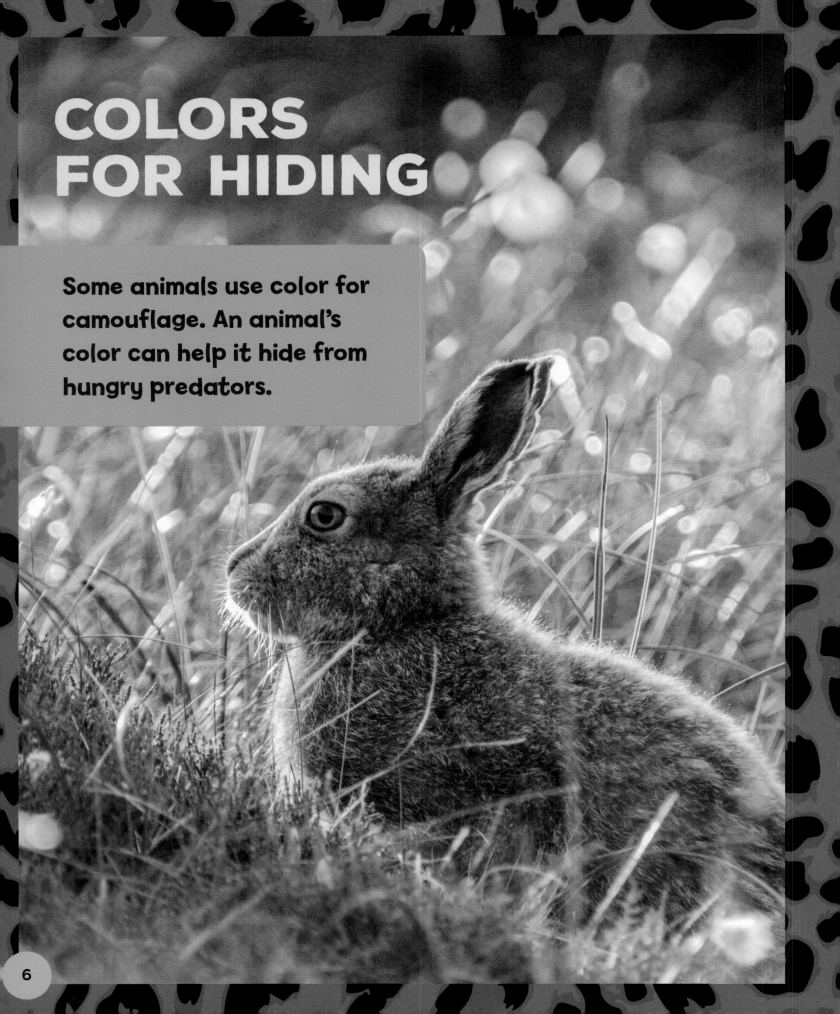

COLORS FOR HIDING

Some animals use color for camouflage. An animal's color can help it hide from hungry predators.

This mountain hare has brown fur during the summer. Then it wears white in winter snow. It's hard for hunting foxes to spot it!

This barred owl's brown-and-white bars blend into trees.

Who-oo-oo-oo would be able to find it? *Not* a predator looking for dinner!

This blue morpho butterfly dazzles from above and looks dull from below. With its wings closed, only brown shows. Where did that blue butterfly go?

COLORS FOR HUNTING

Sometimes camouflage helps animals hunt.

This leopard slinks through dappled trees and grasses.

Prey doesn't see the leopard coming—until the leopard pounces!

This pink-and-white orchid mantis looks like a flower. But it is not hiding.

Instead, this animal tricks other insects. It looks so much like a flower that hungry bugs buzz right in to sip nectar. *Zap!* The mantis snags a snack.

COLORS THAT SAY LOOK AT ME!

Colors can attract a mate.

These male guppies flash bright tails
and scales . . . sky blue, pumpkin orange,
and sunflower yellow. Their colors tell
female guppies, "**Look at me!**"

This peacock's tail feathers explode in blue and aqua. He uses his colors to get attention. When a peacock fans his tail, female birds notice.

Have you ever heard of the peacock . . .
spider? When this male peacock spider
wants to find a mate, he wiggles and
waves his legs. Then he raises his neon
blue-and-orange flap. Female peacock
spiders love his flashy dance.

COLORS THAT SAY STAY AWAY!

Colors can also scare off predators.

These poison dart frogs are wearing banana yellow and sunset orange.

Their colors shout, "Don't eat me. You will get sick if you do!"

This sunny-yellow octopus sports about sixty blue rings. Isn't that cheerful?

Not really. Those rings are a warning. They light up just before the octopus bites. And one poisonous bite is deadly.

The Gila monster also has a poisonous bite. Look at its black-and-coral design. Its bright colors warn, **"Stay away, or you'll be sorry!"**

We look at colorful animals and see beauty. But colors also help animals survive. Take a look at the animal colors around you. What colors can you see?

MANY COLORS

Almond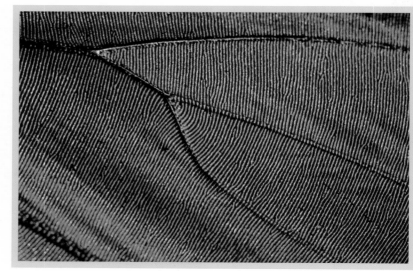

Blue Bell

Wow! Look at these colors and patterns. Can you match them to the animals in this book?

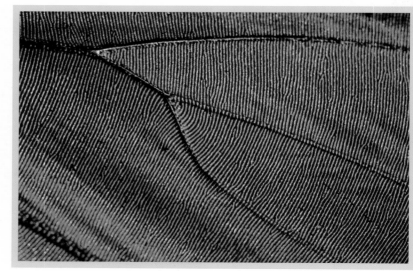

Vivid Tangerine

Antique Brass

Aquamarine

Beaver

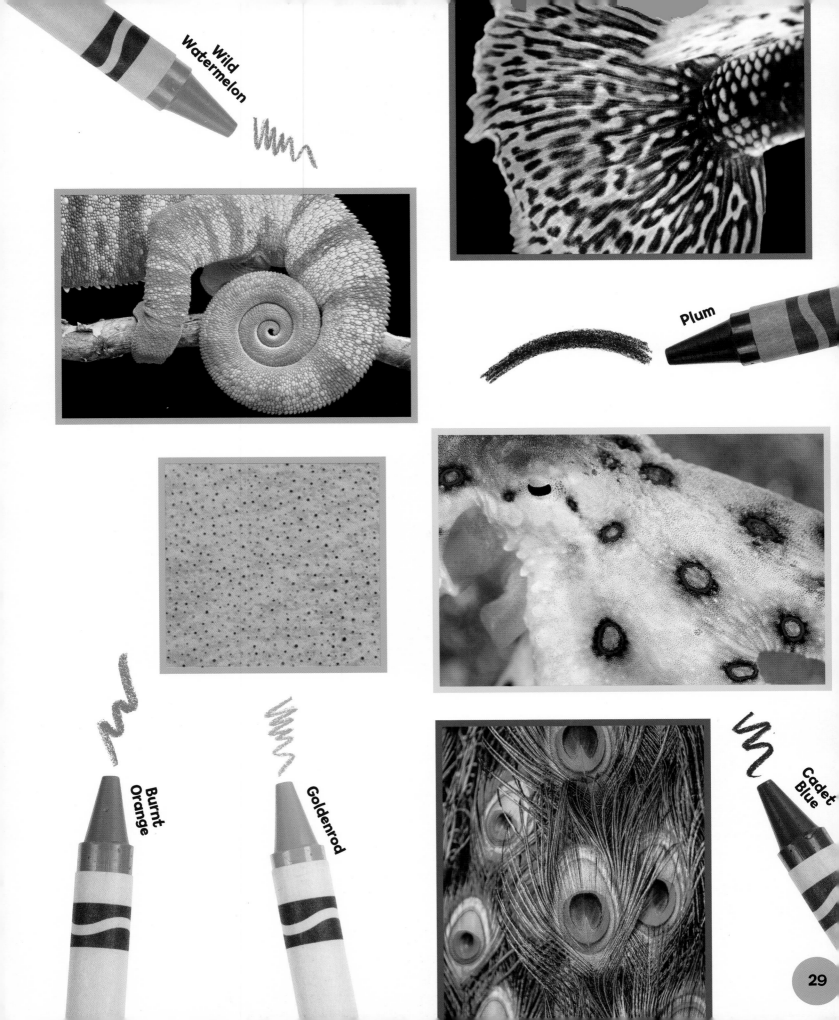

Wild
Watermelon

Plum

Burnt
Orange

Goldenrod

Cadet
Blue

GLOSSARY

camouflage: an animal's color or pattern that blends in with its surroundings

dappled: having small patches of light or dark

mate: a partner

nectar: a sweet liquid made by plants

poisonous: producing something dangerous or deadly

predators: animals that eat other animals

prey: an animal that is hunted or killed by another animal for food

slinks: moves along in a sneaky way

survive: stay alive

threatened: in danger

TO LEARN MORE

Books

Algarra, Alejandro. *Why Are Animals Different Colors?* Hauppauge, NY: Barron's Educational Series, 2016.

Belback, Elsie. *Hidden in Plain Sight: Animal Camouflage*. North Mankato, MN: Rourke Educational Media, 2015.

Keating, Jess. *Pink Is for Blobfish: Discovering the World's Perfectly Pink Animals*. New York: Alfred A. Knopf, 2016.

Websites

National Geographic Kids—Wacky Weekend: Hidden Animals
http://kids.nationalgeographic.com/explore/wacky-weekend/hidden
-animals/#ww-camouflage-owl-reveal.jpg

Seasonal Camouflage
https://www.crayola.com/lesson-plans/seasonal-camouflage-lesson-plan/

Wonderopolis—"Do Animals Play Hide and Seek?"
http://wonderopolis.org/wonder/do-animals-play-hide-and-seek

INDEX

PHOTO ACKNOWLEDGMENTS

The images in this book are used with the permission of: SOMMAI/Shutterstock.com, pp. 1 (top), 30; Johannes Kornelius/Shutterstock.com, p. 1 (bottom); Dirk Ercken/Shutterstock.com, p. 2; Annaev/Shutterstock.com, p. 3; Cathy Keifer/Shutterstock.com, pp. 4–5; © Alex Hyde/Minden Pictures, p. 5 (inset); Phil.Tinkler/Shutterstock.com, p. 6; Peter Wey/Shutterstock.com, p. 7; © Scott Walmsley/Dreamstime.com, pp. 8–9; Romet6/Shutterstock.com, pp. 10–11; davemhuntphotography/Shutterstock.com, p. 11 (inset); Mark Alberhasky/Science Faction/Getty Images, pp. 12–13; Thomas Marent/Minden Pictures/Getty Images, pp. 14–15; bluehand/Shutterstock.com, pp. 16–17; Tereza Wilson/Shutterstock.com, pp. 18–19; © Adam Fletcher/Minden Pictures, pp. 20 (inset), 20–21; Kletr/Shutterstock.com, p. 22; © Matthijs Kuijpers/Dreamstime.com, p. 23; Reinhard Dirscherl/WaterFrame/Getty Images, pp. 24–25; © Farinoza/Dreamstime.com, pp. 26–27; Jared Hobb/All Canada Photos/Getty Images, p. 26 (inset); Andrew Parkinson/The Image Bank/Getty Images, p. 28 (top left); ethylalkohol/Shutterstock.com, p. 28 (middle right); wanchai/Shutterstock.com, p. 28 (bottom); Napat/Shutterstock.com, p. 29 (top right); © Chris Mattison/Minden Pictures, p. 29 (top left); © Mark Moffett/Minden Pictures, p. 29 (middle left); © Constantinos Petrinos/Minden Pictures, p. 29 (middle right); Anna_G/Shutterstock.com, p. 29 (bottom); hfng/Shutterstock.com, p. 31. Design elements: vectorob/Shutterstock.com (zebra print); TabitaZn/Shutterstock.com (leopard print).

Cover: hfng/Shutterstock.com (peacock); Eric Isselee/Shutterstock.com (frog); Johannes Kornelius/Shutterstock.com (orange fish); geraldb/Shutterstock.com (leopard); SOMMAI/Shutterstock.com (yellow fish); Annaev/Shutterstock.com (butterflies); MarkBridger/Moment/Getty Images (chameleon).